In association with

unicef 🐦
United Nations Children's Fund

Y4

A life like mine

DK

A Dorling Kindersley Book

DK

A PENGUIN COMPANY
LONDON, NEW YORK, MUNICH,
MELBOURNE, AND DELHI

UNICEF (NY) Consultant Arati Rao
Senior Editor Amanda Rayner
Senior Art Editor Claire Penny
Project Editor Zahavit Shalev
Art Editors Laura Roberts, Venice Shone
Researcher Lisa Magloff
Design Assistant Abbie Collinson

Design Consultant Jane Bull
Managing Editor Sue Leonard
Managing Art Editor Cathy Chesson
Category Publisher Mary Ling
Picture Research Angela Anderson, Sarah Pownall
Jacket Design Sophia Tampakopoulos
Production Silvia La Greca Bertacchi, Shivani Pandey
DTP Designer Almudena Díaz

All maps used in this book are artistic representations.
They do not reflect a position by UNICEF or Dorling Kindersley on the
legal status of any country or territory or the delimitation of any frontiers.
Dotted line represents approximately the Line of Control in Jammu and Kashmir
agreed upon by India and Pakistan. The final status of Jammu and
Kashmir has not yet been agreed upon by the parties.

Every effort has been made to ensure that the statistics in this book are up to date
at the time of going to press.

First published in Great Britain in 2002 by
Dorling Kindersley Limited
80 Strand, London WC2R 0RL

2 4 6 8 10 9 7 5 3 1

Copyright © 2002 Dorling Kindersley Limited
First paperback edition 2006

A CIP catalogue record for this book
is available from the British Library

Paperback edition ISBN 1-4053-1460-5
Hardback edition ISBN 0-7513-3982-2

Colour reproduction by GRB Editrice, S.r.l.,Verona
Printed and bound by Leo in China

See our complete
catalogue at

www.dk.com

unicef

United Nations Children's Fund

There are millions of children, leading different lives, all over the world.
You speak different languages, look different, and face all manner of challenges every day. However, although you live thousands of kilometres apart, in many respects your needs and hopes are alike.

It is for this reason that the Convention on the Rights of the Child has been drawn up and accepted by almost every country of the world. It promises essential rights to every one of the world's children. Each child, boys and girls equally, has a right to education, health care, food, shelter, play, and protection – and much more.

A Life Like Mine records the courage, energy, joy, and optimism of children from all over the world. Some of the children in this book enjoy every privilege in their lives, others have been deprived of some of their basic rights. I hope you enjoy meeting them and that you discover the similarities between their lives and your own.

You are special. You deserve protection and support as you grow to adulthood. You are part of the present, but all of the future.

Jemima Khan
UNICEF UK Special Representative

———— About UNICEF ————

UNICEF's mission is to create conditions that enable children to live happy, healthy, and dignified lives.
Every aspect of UNICEF's work – ranging from programmes to improve children's health and education to protecting children from violence, exploitation, and disasters – is guided by the Convention on the Rights of the Child.

www.unicef.org

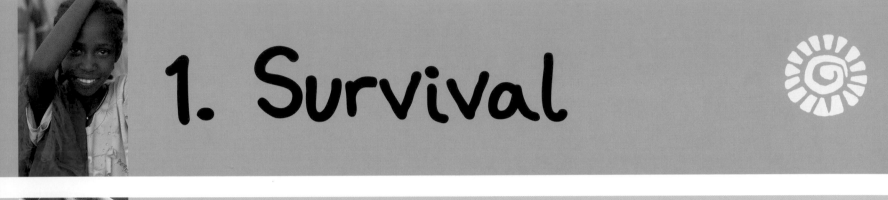

1. Survival

2. Development

3. Protection

4. Participation

Contents

Where do they live?

In this book you will meet children from around the world. Although they seem very different, they all share one goal – they want to lead a good life. In the following pages you'll learn about their lives, thoughts, and hopes for the future.

Natalie

Natalie is nine years old. She lives in Bedfordshire in the UK. Meet her on page 42.

Taralyn

Taralyn is 10 years old. She lives near Seattle, Washington, USA. Meet Taralyn on page 120.

USA

Isa

Isa is 10 years old. He lives in Sierra Leone. Meet him on page 88.

COLOMBIA

CJ

CJ is 13 years old. He lives in Atlanta, Georgia, USA. Meet CJ on page 96.

Children around the World

There are over 6 billion people in the world. More than 2 billion of them are under 18.

More than 210 million children aged 5–14 work. More than half of those are involved in dangerous work or work full-time.

Nearly 11 million children under five die each year, mostly from preventable diseases.

Mayerly

Mayerly is now 18. She lives in Bogotá, Colombia. Meet her on page 126.

Ivana

Ivana is 12 years old. She lives in Pristina in Yugoslavia. Meet her on page 72.

Eli

Eli is 15. He lives at Yemin Orde Youth Village in Israel. Meet him on page 112.

Nadin

Nadin is 11. She lives in Kalandia camp in the Occupied Palestinian Territory. Meet her on page 34.

Najaha & Abdisukri

Najaha is 10 and Abdisukri is nine. They live in Tilburg in the Netherlands. Meet them on page 108.

Maria

Maria is nine. She lives in Kabul, Afghanistan. Meet her on page 54.

Nou

Nou is nine. She lives in Ponsavanh in Laos. Meet her on page 16.

Mahasin

Mahasin is nine years old. She lives in Tambisco, Sudan. Meet her on page 32.

UK
NETHERLANDS
YUGOSLAVIA
ISRAEL AND OCCUPIED PALESTINIAN TERRITORY
AFGHANISTAN
BANGLADESH
INDIA
LAOS
SIERRA LEONE
SUDAN
RWANDA
SOUTH AFRICA
AUSTRALIA

Sbongile

Sbongile is 10 years old. She lives in Cape Town, South Africa. Meet her on page 52.

Vincent

Vincent is 15 years old. He lives in Rwanda. Meet him on page 24.

Sibasish

Sibasish is 13 years old. He lives in Kolkata, India. Meet him on page 124.

Arif

Arif is 12. He lives in Dhaka in Bangladesh. Meet him on page 80.

Michael

Michael is six. He lives on Lake Torrens Station in Australia. Meet him on page 62.

1. Survival

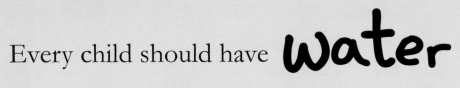

Every child should have **water** that is safe to drink near to their home.

Every child should have enough nourishing **food** to eat so they can grow and thrive.

Survival – noun; to survive – verb **1** to remain alive; continue to live. **2** to continue to function or manage in spite of some adverse circumstance or hardship; hold up; endure.

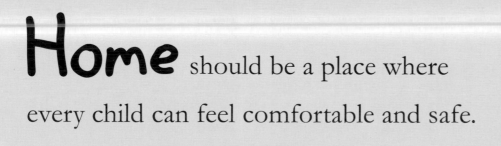

Home should be a place where every child can feel comfortable and safe.

Every child should have access to **health** care in order to lead a full and active life.

Every child should have

Water

washing, ceremony, drinking,

The water of life

Without water there would be no life on Earth.
Water is our planet's most precious possession.
A human being can survive only a few days without water.
We use water in so many different ways without even thinking
about it. Some of us just turn the tap on and water gushes
But not everybody in the world can take water for granted.

growing food, swimming, playing

How much water is there?

More than 70% of the world is covered in water.

Imagine waking up tomorrow and finding that there were no taps. **What would you do?**

- **Like many people** in the world, you would have to collect the water you needed from a river, lake, well, pump, or communal tap.

- **Water keeps us alive.** We use it to drink, to grow food, and to wash. It's also essential for building houses and running factories.

- **97 per cent of the world's water is salty** sea water and cannot be used. Most of the fresh water in the world is too difficult to reach because it's underground or in icebergs. Only 1 per cent of the Earth's fresh water is available – but that's still plenty for our needs.

How much Water do you use?

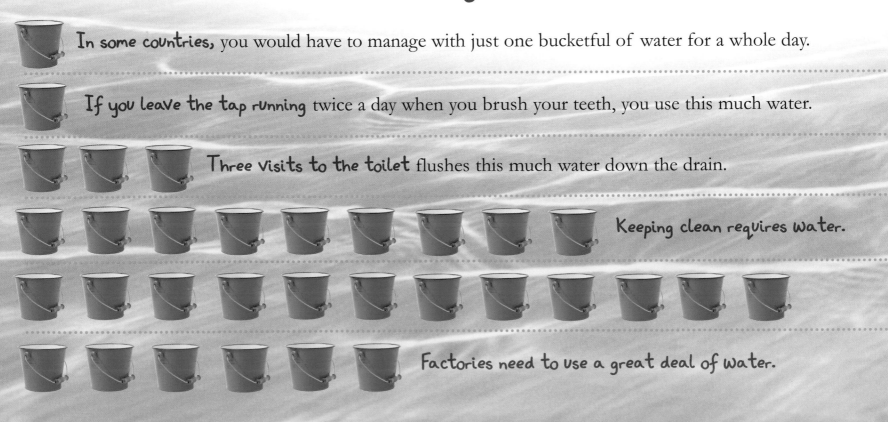

In some countries, you would have to manage with just one bucketful of water for a whole day.

If you leave the tap running twice a day when you brush your teeth, you use this much water.

Three visits to the toilet flushes this much water down the drain.

Keeping clean requires water.

Factories need to use a great deal of water.

Even the 1 per cent of fresh water available on our planet is sometimes unsafe to drink.

So is there enough water for everyone?
Yes! But there are still problems...

- **Too little rain** Enough rainwater falls every day to cover the land in a layer 80 cm (31 in) deep. That should be plenty for everyone. The problem is that it falls more in some areas than in others.

- **Bad water** Every day 14,000 people die because the water they use contains dangerous chemicals or untreated sewage. Diarrhoea, caused by dirty water and dirty conditions, kills more than 1 million children a year.

- **Too much rain** Many fertile parts of the world are prone to flooding. Floods destroy people's homes and often cause the water supply to become dirty. This makes it easy for diseases to spread.

- **Dry deserts** 14 per cent of the world's surface is desert and the desert is growing all the time. Deserts have little or no rainfall. People have to walk miles to get water for themselves, their animals, and their crops.

Water facts

Believe it or not, 75 per cent of you is water!

You would probably die after three days without water.

Water makes up 50 per cent of your bones.

That means water for **drinking**, **washing**, and **cooking**.

That's **a whole day's supply** for some people.

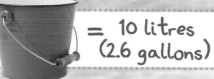

= 10 litres (2.6 gallons)

This much water **fills a bath**.

Washing machines guzzle all this water for one load of laundry.

We can't drink sea water because it's too salty.

It took this amount of water to make **the shoes you are wearing**.

Watery tales

These children are lucky in having access to clean, safe running water. Yet most of them have to collect it daily for their families – a difficult and time-consuming task.

Afghanistan Two boys collect water from a hand pump. Villages in this region are affected by drought, so these pumps are a lifeline. Local people have received hygiene education and been trained in maintaining the hand pumps.

This village in Afghanistan was bombed during a war in the 1980s. Even in 2002 it had still not been rebuilt.

A bucket to carry the water home

India Two girls carry containers to a communal water source. They will fill them up with water and then take them home. The girls use as many containers as they can for each trip, and carry the biggest pots on their heads and the other containers in their hands. Their heads are cushioned from the metal pots by a piece of cloth.

... A 10-litre (2.6-gallon) bucket of water weighs 10 kg (22 lbs). That's quite heavy. In fact it's about the same weight as a one-year-old child!

The Netherlands Najaha helps herself to a glass of water from the tap in her kitchen. She's the only person on this page who doesn't have to leave her house to get water.

... How many taps and sinks are there in your home? How would your life change if there were only one tap in your home? What about if you had to collect water from outside your home? Or from a few streets away?

Jamaica A girl fills a bucket with water from a community standpipe. The standpipe is not as convenient as having a tap in your house, but it's better than having to collect water from a river or a lake. When people come to collect their water, they also share news and gossip.

... Before it reaches the standpipe, the water is pumped out of the ground. Then it must be treated to remove dirt and germs so it will be safe to drink. Otherwise, it is no safer than river water.

Water gushes out!

Nou

Two years ago, a pump was installed in Nou's village in Laos. Previously, people collected water from a stream. It was not safe and often made them ill.

BEFORE THE PUMP

A nearby stream provided all the water for Nou's village. The water was not safe, but it was all the villagers had. For three months of the year, the stream dried up. People dug into the stream bed for water, but it was always muddy.

... "Now that there is safe water to drink, people have stopped getting sick and can spend less time and money on visits to the doctor."

COLLECTING WATER

Children in Laos collect water for their families. Nou and her friends used to make many trips to the stream, sometimes missing school.

... "I had my own buckets, which were smaller than the ones my older sister used."

MYANMAR
CHINA
VIET NAM
LAOS
THAILAND
CAMBODIA

Laos

Mountainous and full of forests, Laos has a monsoon climate. This means both droughts and floods occur, depending on the season.

THE JOURNEY

The walk to collect water included a steep hill and a rickety bridge. It took 10 minutes to get there, but 20 minutes returning with heavy buckets.

... "I used to get water from the stream twice a day. I would walk with my friends. We could talk while we went even though the buckets were heavy."

MORE TIME

Now that the pump is in the centre of the village, everyone has more time than before – Nou to play, and her mother to help in the fields.

... "We can get water so easily. I can go and bring back a fresh bucket whenever I want."

LAUNDRY

People still use the river to do laundry, but going to the toilet is simpler and more hygienic, thanks to a new covered toilet built by Nou's father and brother.

... "The roof and walls of our toilet are made of leaves and thatch, and it's not far from the house."

SCHOOL GARDEN

The village has a new feature now. A garden was impractical before because it was too far to go to collect water for the plants. That is not a problem now because the village pump is actually in the school yard.

... "We have a school garden with flowers in it. We water it every day."

"Life is better now!"

Every child should have

food

survival, growth, good health,

Food is our fuel

We eat in order to survive.

We enjoy the tastes, smells, and textures of food.

Most celebrations and holidays involve eating together.

While people in rich parts of the world are dying from diseases caused by overeating, many in poorer parts of the world are struggling just to get enough food to survive.

strength, energy, feasting

Why do we need food?

Every day, 14% of people in the world go to bed hungry.

14%

Have you ever tried to study or play when you were **hungry**?

● **When children don't get enough food**, they don't have the energy to work, play, or learn. Their bodies and brains don't grow as well as they should, and they are more likely to suffer from diseases.

● **Malnutrition** means not getting enough of the food you need. Every year, millions of children die from diseases made worse by malnutrition.

● **When there is a shortage of food**, some parents in some countries will feed their sons better than their daughters, resulting in worse malnutrition among girls.

Proteins

Vitamins and minerals

What happens when we do not eat a balanced diet?

One child in four does not get enough protein or calories.

Filling foods like rice, noodles, bread, and cereals are called carbohydrates.

One person in two does not get enough vitamins and minerals.

Foods containing sugars and fats can taste really good.

Eat good food!

Why do people go hungry?

• **Environmental problems**, such as drought, floods, and deforestation, destroy the soil, making it hard to grow food. Problems get worse when people farm land with damaged soil.

• **War** forces people away from their homes and off their land so it's hard to plant crops and distribute food that is grown. During war, governments spend money on weapons instead of food.

• **Over-grazing** by animals damages the land and the soil, so crops cannot grow. Over-fishing affects not just the number of fish in the sea, but other animals and plants in the food chain.

• **Some people don't have money** to buy all the food they need, or enough land and tools to grow it themselves. As food becomes less available, the price goes up even more.

Many poor people have to spend almost all of their money on food, leaving very little left over for other necessities.

A good idea?

Why can't we just send hungry people our extra food?

It would prevent people dying, but it wouldn't solve the reasons why hunger happens.

Governments need to make sure everyone has a way to grow or buy the food they need.

Carbohydrates

Each child is sick for **many days** each year.

Without them, children have **no energy** to get through the day.

This **weakens** the body's resistance to **disease**.

But too much can make us **overweight** and **unhealthy**.

Stay healthy and happy!

Sugars and fats

What's cooking?

A staple food is the one that our meals are based around. Whether it's bread, rice, noodles, or potatoes, when we see or smell it we know we won't be hungry for long.

UK Some people like to have a big Sunday lunch. A traditional main course for this meal might consist of roast beef, roast potatoes, Yorkshire pudding, vegetables, and gravy.

... This meal is eaten at a table using knives and forks. English people often chat during a big meal.

Viet Nam There are lots of rivers and lakes in Southeast Asia, so people eat plenty of fish.

... In Asia, most meals contain either rice or noodles. Vietnamese people eat food from a bowl using chopsticks.

Bangladesh Typical flavourings for food include salt, coriander, turmeric, cumin, chilli powder, garlic, onions, and chillies.

... In Bangladesh, people eat using only their right hand. People don't talk much while they eat.

Mozambique *Fufu* is the focus of most meals in Mozambique. Making *fufu* is always energetic work. You have to boil the grains, then pound them hard, and stir it till you get a smooth paste.

Fufu can be made of maize, sweet potato, or plantain (a type of savoury banana). Elsewhere in Africa, it is sometimes called sadza or ugali.

Grains of maize (actual size)

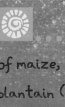

Fufu

Vincent

Fifteen-year-old Vincent lives in Rwanda. His mother and father are dead, so Vincent looks after his younger sisters and brother. He does many of the household chores, including growing and buying the food that the family eats.

PREPARING LUNCH
Donata Uwamahoro, Vincent's 14-year-old sister, is responsible for cooking the midday meal while Vincent is at school.

"My older brother is 32. He lives nearby with a family of his own."

Rwanda

Rwanda's temperate climate is good for farming. Most people eat what they grow, though some grow tea, coffee, and other crops to sell.

CONGO, DEM. REP   UGANDA   TANZANIA

RWANDA

BURUNDI

BANANAS AND GOATS

Vincent grows bananas on his land. He also keeps some goats in an enclosure. They provide manure for the crops.

.... "I get up when it is light. I don't have a watch. My first task is to cut some grass to feed to our goats."

VEGETABLE PATCH

Vincent's brother helps him to weed the cabbage patch. A local organization gave Vincent advice about growing vegetables so he also grows tomatoes and sweet potatoes.

.... "We used to earn a little from our coffee bushes, but they have stopped producing beans. I make money from doing odd jobs now."

WORKING WITH WOOD

Vincent takes carpentry lessons at a day centre for orphans run by a local organization.

.... "I wish to become a carpenter so that I can earn a living by making beds and other furniture."

ALL FIRED UP

Vincent's sister does most of the cooking, but her brothers help her to light the fire.

.... "We have one meal a day. I eat at school, the others eat at home."

Every child should have a

home

Warm, cool, dry, safe, shelter,

Home sweet home

Our homes protect us from the weather.
At home we feel safe, comfortable, and relaxed.
A home can be built anywhere and out of anything.
Around the world, people live in all sorts of homes
including houses, flats, caravans, caves, houseboats,
treehouses, and tents.

privacy, space, comfort, peace

Where do people live?

A home is more than a building. It is a place where you can be **secure**, **safe**, **healthy**, and **happy**.

It doesn't matter what a house looks like, but to be a good home for children, a house needs to provide:

- **Protection** from the weather, injury, smoke, and pollution
- **A safe water supply** in the house or nearby
- **Sturdy walls** that cannot catch fire easily
- **Sanitary ways** to get rid of human waste and rubbish
- **Safe food storage** and preparation
- **Enough room** for everyone living there
- **Adults** who can care for children.

There is not **enough** affordable housing,

- Nearly half of the world's population lives in cities.
- 250 million people in cities do not have safe piped water.
- 400 million people in cities have no toilet or latrine.
- At least 600 million people live in city slums or shantytowns.

More than 20 million families in the world's cities are homeless.

Not everyone is homeless for the same reason.
There are many causes of homelessness.

- **War and violence** force people out of their homes. Over half of the world's refugees are children. Some children run away from home because of violence.

- When there is **no work**, people leave the countryside and move to the cities. This makes the cities very crowded and housing there is even more expensive.

- **Natural disasters**, such as droughts, floods, volcanos, and storms, can destroy homes. After a disaster, there might not be any money to rebuild houses.

- **There is not enough cheap housing** for all the people who need it. The unemployed or those earning very little sometimes end up on the streets.

There are lots of different types of houses

In the hot deserts of Tunisia, some people live in underground houses, where it is cool.

On the rivers of Hong Kong and Thailand, people sometimes live on river-boats.

so some people have to live in bad conditions.

- A third of all city dwellers live in substandard housing.

- That means the poorest families have nowhere to wash. Many have to buy water from expensive water sellers.

- Many families have to share a toilet. They face a bleak future exposed to unsanitary conditions that breed disease.

- **1.3 billion** people have inadequate housing.

A place to live

Homes differ enormously around the world. There are city homes and country homes, homes in hot climates and in cold climates, homes on or near water, and homes on or near mountains. What makes a home a home? The people who live in it.

Turkey Our earliest ancestors probably found shelter from the sun, wind, and rain in caves. Today some people still choose to live in a cave or to use a cave as the basis for their houses. This home is built into the side of a cave. The thick walls help to keep the home cool in summer and warm in winter.

... The most convenient thing about a cave dwelling is that you don't have to build your home from scratch because the cave is already there.

China A family sit in their wooden houseboat moored in the shallows near a fishing village in Fujian Province. Living on the river is practical both for fishing and for selling the fish you catch, so it's often fishermen and their families who live in homes like these.

... When you live on a houseboat, you soon get used to the slight rocking motion of the water and the cramped conditions. Children brought up on a houseboat learn to swim and to behave responsibly around the water from an early age.

Laos People in Laos weave panels out of rattan (a kind of grass). It only takes one day for the panels to be lashed together to form a house. However, the panels do need to be replaced regularly.

. . . In the rainy season, it can get very muddy. That's why this house is built on stilts. The area on the right is a pen where the family keep their pigs. The pigs don't mind the mud!

UK TJ's family work in a travelling circus in southeast England. They are on the road for most of the year. They live in this trailer, which they bought in the USA. It is very comfortable and has a washing machine and a microwave.

. . . The children of people who travel go to many different schools. They keep a record book, which they take to each school.

Rwanda Vincent lives here with his two sisters and his brother. Their two-room house is made of sunbaked mud brick. Vincent and his family built their own house, with help from their neighbours and friends, who pitched in to make bricks and construct the house.

. . . When there is no money for expensive building materials, people use whatever materials are available. Thick mud bricks are practical in hot, dry climates, because they keep the house cool.

Mahasin

Nomadic cattle herders like Mahasin and her family don't live in one place but move about to find fresh grass for their cattle. They use the milk from their cows to make butter, which they sell. Moving around is an adventure, and Mahasin loves her way of life.

MOVEABLE HOME
The family's home is made out of twigs and sticks woven together. Twice a year, when the community migrates, the hut is taken apart and the materials transported on camels and oxen so it can be rebuilt in a new location.

"Me, my mother, and my sisters sleep in the family hut. The men in the family sleep in an open hut where they can keep an eye on the cattle."

Sudan
The landscape of Sudan includes desert in the north, tropical forests and grassy plains in the south, and swamps in the centre. It is the largest country in Africa.

NOMADIC LIFE

Mahasin's family moves frequently in order to find grass and water for their cattle. All of Mahasin's personal belongings need to fit into one small trunk.

 … "The thing I like best in life is when we move. Wherever we go with our cattle, people treat us with respect and often help us. We can go everywhere we want."

STAPLE FOOD

Mahasin likes to help her mother and sisters with the cooking and cleaning. The family's staple food is called *asida*. It is a dish of vegetables and grains mixed with spices.

Mahasin helps her mother to wash up.

TRAVELLING SCHOOL

Mahasin attends a special school for nomadic children. There are about 50 children at the school, but students change all the time because of constant migrations.

… "We learn the Arabic language, religion, and geography. Our teacher's name is Fadul Osman. He always travels with us. He is one of us."

BASKET WEAVING

When Mahasin is not studying, she helps her family to look after their cattle and weaves baskets for the family to use.

Mahasin's necklace is called a *khannakh*.

A DESERT HOPPING GAME

Mahasin and her friends play a traditional game called *arikkia*.

Nadin

Nadin and her family live in a refugee camp in the West Bank run by the United Nations. Her family fled from their original town of Malha, historical Palestine, after the 1948 Arab-Israeli war.

A FAMILY HOME

Nadin, her parents, two sisters, and a brother all live on just the lower floor of the house. Nadin's grandparents, aunt, uncle, and their children all live on the upper floor.

... "My family has been living in the camp for more than 53 years, since it was set up in 1949. My grandmother was six when she moved here from the town of Malha."

AT PLAY

There are few places in the camp for girls to play, so Nadin plays either indoors or on the street in front of the house.

Occupied Palestinian Territory

The Occupied Palestinian Territory is in two separate parts – the West Bank and Gaza. Israel occupied the land during the 1967 war.

WEST BANK

GAZA

ISRAEL

JORDAN

EGYPT

TIME FOR BED
Nadin shares her bedroom with eight-year-old Wafa. The rest of the family sleeps in the family room.

... "I love my sister Wafa though we argue a lot because she is very talkative. She wants to be famous and appear on TV."

Nadin and her sister Wafa and brother Mohammed

FAMILY TIES
Nadin is very close to everyone in her family. Because she is the eldest, she helps her mother to look after her younger sister, Hala, who is only two years old.

... "We eat a popular Palestinian dish called musakhan. It is made of bread, onion, chicken, and spices all fried up together."

Musakhan

Olives

HELPING AT HOME
After she gets home from school, Nadin helps her mother with chores such as sweeping the floor and dusting the furniture.

NOT SO DIFFERENT
Palestinian food is similar to that of other countries in the region including Jordan, Israel, Turkey, Greece, Iran, and Iraq.

... "My biggest wish is to go back to Malha, our original city. I also wish for peace between Israelis and Palestinians."

Every child deserves a

healthy life

strong bones, healthy teeth,

Staying well

It's best not to get ill in the first place.
Vaccinations can protect us against some diseases.
Good hygiene and a healthy diet can help us avoid others.
But sometimes people become ill. When that happens,
they may need the help of doctors, medicines, and
hospitals to get well again.

fitness, hygiene, immunization

What do you need to stay healthy?

Good health is the most precious thing you have.

- **To stay healthy**, you need good food and safe water, somewhere to wash yourself, a place to go to the toilet, vaccines, health care, and a way to dispose of your rubbish safely.

- **When you get ill**, you need to be able to see someone, such as a doctor or a nurse or a health worker, who can help you to get better.

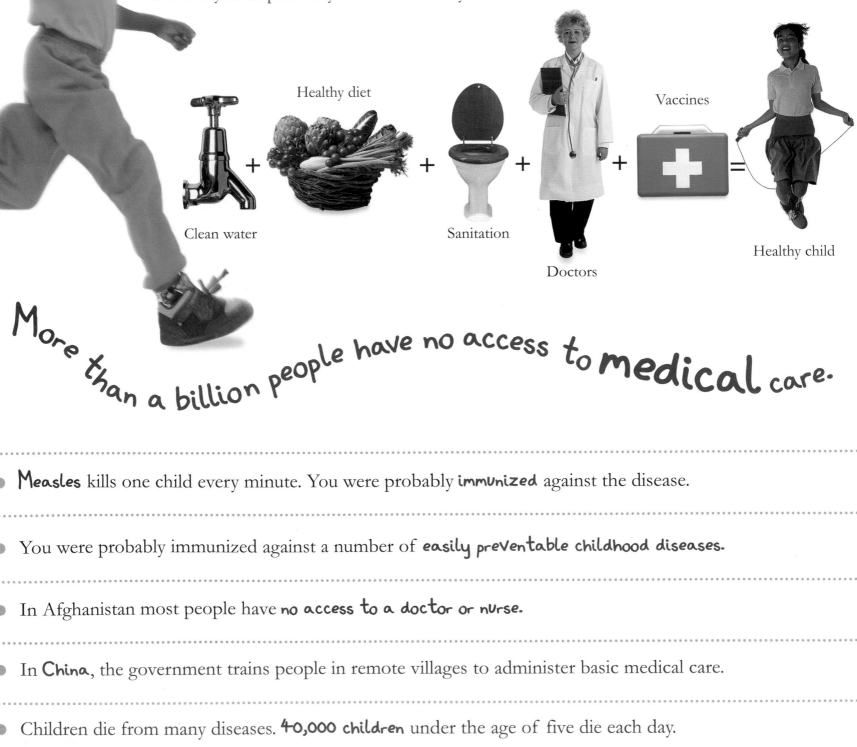

Clean water + Healthy diet + Sanitation + Doctors + Vaccines = Healthy child

More than a billion people have no access to medical care.

- **Measles** kills one child every minute. You were probably **immunized** against the disease.

- You were probably immunized against a number of **easily preventable childhood diseases.**

- In Afghanistan most people have **no access to a doctor or nurse.**

- In **China**, the government trains people in remote villages to administer basic medical care.

- Children die from many diseases. **40,000 children** under the age of five die each day.

Some of the world's deadliest illnesses can be easily and cheaply prevented.

• **Malaria** is caused by mosquitoes. It affects up to 500 million people each year. Yet it can be prevented by sleeping under a mosquito net and by getting rid of mosquito breeding areas.

• **Malnutrition** affects 150 million children. It leaves them weak and unable to fight disease. Malnutrition can be prevented by having enough healthy food to eat and basic health care.

• **Diarrhoea** causes dehydration, which kills more than 1 million children a year. It can be avoided by access to clean food and water. A person can be cured with a 5p packet of rehydration salts.

• **Measles** rarely kills healthy children. However, in developing countries, it kills nearly 1 million children each year. It can be prevented with a vaccine that costs 7p per dose.

The tragedy of AIDS

In sub-Saharan Africa, millions of children have been orphaned by AIDS. Many more are having their education disrupted because their teachers are dying of the disease.

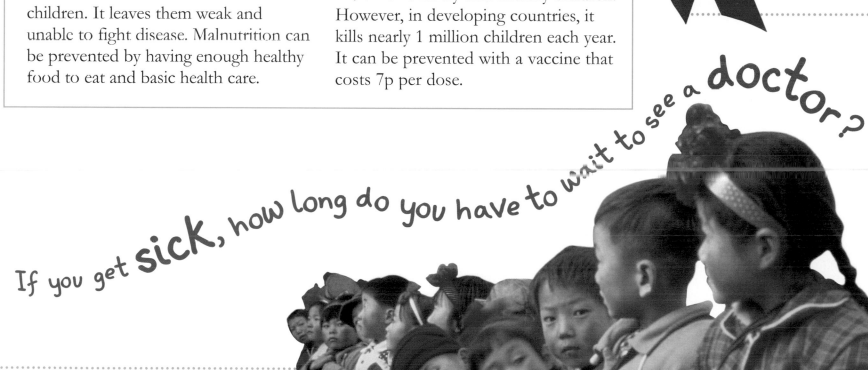

If you get **sick**, how long do you have to wait to see a *doctor*?

In Africa, **50 per cent** were not.

Sadly, **34 million** children are not.

In Italy most people do.

They're called **barefoot doctors**.

Malnutrition is what kills them.

Health for life

Health care is vital in the early years when children are growing fast and are exposed to a lot of diseases. Healthy children have a much better chance of growing up to be healthy adults.

Angola A girl with a respiratory infection is examined by a doctor in a hospital in Luanda, the capital. Finally, after years of fighting in Angola, the government, assisted by UNICEF, is able to improve basic education and health care.

... All children need regular health check-ups just to make sure that everything is all right and no problems are developing.

India A girl smiles as she carries a clay jug of water to her home in Tamil Nadu. Sadly, dirty drinking water is responsible for many preventable deaths, especially in babies and young children.

... Pots like these keep water fresh and cool. However, a safe supply of tap water would be much more convenient for everyone.

Bangladesh This two-year-old girl has plenty to smile about as she splashes clean bath water. The bath water in her plastic basin came from a new hand pump.

... Using a river or lake for washing or for going to the toilet makes the water unsafe for drinking.

Zambia Fruit and vegetables are rich in vitamins and minerals that help us recover from diseases, and even prevent us from getting ill in the first place. Different foods contain different nutrients, so it's important to have a balanced diet.

... Our bodies cannot store most vitamins, so in order to stay healthy we need to eat fresh foods every day.

China A girl takes a polio vaccine at a UNICEF-assisted clinic. By vaccinating as many children as possible, the World Health Organization, UNICEF, and other partners hope to have freed the world from polio by 2005.

... The polio vaccine is quick and easy to take. The child just swallows the medicine! However, to be totally effective, you need to take it on four separate occasions.

Natalie

Natalie suffers from eczema and from asthma, a condition affecting the tubes that carry air in and out of her lungs. There is no cure, but fortunately, Natalie is able to manage her condition and leads a very active life.

ECZEMA

Many asthmatics suffer from a skin condition called eczema. Natalie has to be careful what her skin comes into contact with. Some things make it break into sores.

Eczema cream

... "I have to cream my skin morning and evening. The hot weather makes my skin itchy. Once I start scratching, I cannot stop and my skin easily bleeds and gets infected."

United Kingdom

Factories and traffic in developed countries, such as the UK, tend to create pollution. This can cause problems for asthmatics. Asthma affects one in eight children in the UK.

SPORTS

Exercise can trigger attacks for some asthma sufferers, but luckily that's not the case for Natalie. In fact, she finds that doing lots of sports has made her chest stronger, so she suffers from fewer colds and asthma attacks.

TRIGGERS

Natalie can't have many soft toys, and she can't have pets or wear wool either because the dust from these can bring on an asthma attack. The family house has no carpets or curtains for the same reason.

DIET

Natalie suffers from food allergies, so she must be careful about what she eats. Milk, cheese, and eggs could make her very ill.

Cheese

Egg

Milk

Spacer device

Reliever spray

Preventer spray

INHALERS

Natalie treats her asthma with two inhaler sprays. She must use her preventer every day to calm her airways. Her reliever opens up her airways if she gets an attack.

... "When I have an asthma attack, my chest feels all light and horrid. Sometimes I cannot stop coughing. That's when I take my reliever to make it easier for me to breathe."

Ice-skates

... "I do gymnastics on Wednesday, swimming on Thursday, netball on Friday, and ice-skating on Saturday! I also like rollerblading and I do it whenever I can outside our house."

2. Development

Education is the right of every child. Education should help children to develop their personality, talents, and abilities. It should also teach them to respect other people.

Development –noun; to develop – verb 1 to bring out the possibilities of. 2 to grow. 3 to mature or evolve.

Every child should have time and somewhere safe to **play**.

All children should be allowed to have privacy if they want

to spend some time on their own.

Every child has the right to

education

numeracy, literacy, stimulation,

School rules!

Human beings are always learning.
School gives you skills such as reading, writing, and maths.
It also develops your personality, talents, and abilities.
Just as importantly, it teaches you your rights and
responsibilities, and guides you so you learn to respect others
and to live peacefully with them.

skills, information, concepts

Why do we need an education?

Do you ever wish you didn't have to go to school? Millions of children around the world can't ever go to school. More than half of them are girls.

• **If you can't read, write, or do simple maths**, it is hard to find a good job, and people may take advantage of you. Without school, it is very difficult to escape poverty. Children who go to school get better jobs when they are older, they live longer, and are healthier.

• **School is more than reading, writing, and maths.** School is a place to learn about self-respect and dignity, and to find out about our rights. School is also where we learn about staying healthy and how to prevent disease.

Why are girls behind boys in literacy?

• **One girl in four** around the world who should be in school full time is not.

• **In sub–Saharan Africa** about 40 per cent of girls are not being educated.

• **In some places,** people do not believe that girls need an education.

• **Some girls are kept at home** to help around the house or to work on the family farm or business.

• **Families that cannot afford** to send all their children to school may send only the boys.

One out of every seven people around the world cannot read or write this sentence.

Why isn't there education for everyone?

- **Some children live in places without schools or teachers.** In some places, there are no schools or not enough qualified teachers. Sometimes there are schools but they can't cater for children with disabilities or special needs.

- **Some work to help support their families.** Parents might only be able to afford an education for some of their children and may need the others to work and bring home a wage. So in one family, some children may go to school and others may not.

- **Some can't afford school fees.** Not all countries provide free education. Even when education is free, parents may not be able to afford the cost of books, school uniforms, and other equipment such as pens or notebooks.

- **Some have no families to help them.** Children who have run away from home or who are orphaned may be sleeping on city streets. They are struggling just to survive, and very few of them manage to get an education.

Nearly **100%** of children in the USA and Europe go to school.

53% of children not in primary school are girls. (**47%** are boys).

Around the world, people are recognizing that the key to improving lives is to educate girls and women.

In poorer countries, only **45%** of girls (and **55%** of boys) go on to secondary school.

550 million women (and **320 million** men) are unable to read or write.

School for all!

Education is the key to a better future for everyone, but for millions of children, going to school is no easy matter. All over the world, governments, non-governmental organizations (NGOs), parents, and children themselves are finding ways to make sure that children receive the vital learning they need to improve their lives.

Bangladesh Until recently, this girl spent her days working in a clothes factory. Then the company she worked for agreed to stop hiring children and to help pay for them to go to school instead. Now she is learning how to read. Informal schools like this give former child workers a chance to escape poverty.

In **North korea** a drought resulted in a food shortage, which meant that millions of children were too hungry to go to school. After aid programmes began supplying food to this nursery school, attendance rose from just 20 per cent to more than 90 per cent.

... It's hard to concentrate on learning if your tummy is rumbling!

✂ ●●● This girl was lucky. Some children have to work, and so miss out on going to school. Schools need to offer these children part-time schooling so they don't miss out altogether.

✂ ●●● Education is so important that when a child cannot go to school, the school must come to the child.

Some **Australian** children living in the outback are hundreds of kilometres from the nearest school. The only way they can study is by talking to their teachers on two-way radios and sending in their homework by post.

Kenya For thousands of orphaned children, like 12-year-old Thomas, education was just a dream until he started attending a UNICEF-assisted centre in Nairobi. The centre provides education, counselling, and skills training to children who are living or working on the streets. For these children, it's much more than just a school – it's a lifeline.

School gives you hope.

✂ ●●● Thomas displays his new skills in arithmetic. He has lived on the streets since he was 10 years old. Receiving an education means he has a brighter future.

UNIFORM
Sbongile wears a white shirt and a navy blue and white tracksuit to school. It has the school badge on it and says "Ellerton".

Sbongile

Just a few years ago, Sbongile could not have attended Ellerton Primary School in South Africa. At that time, the apartheid laws prevented black and white people from mixing. Those laws have now been completely abolished.

JOURNEY
Ellerton is near the beach at Sea Point, a long way from Sbongile's home. Sbongile's mother wakes her up at 4.30 a.m. so she can be picked up for the journey to school at 5.50 a.m.

"A driver collects 16 of us from our houses. I am the first one he collects and then he collects the other children. I get to school at 7.30 a.m."

"I take books, pencils, and a reading book to school. Sometimes I take sandwiches, tuna, and polony (processed meat) or cheese and bacon and egg. Sometimes my mother gives me money to buy a pie or a samosa from the tuck shop."

South Africa
At the southern tip of the African continent lies South Africa. The country is rich in natural resources including coal, tin, iron ore, gold, and diamonds.

BOTSWANA
NAMIBIA
LESOTHO
SOUTH AFRICA

LANGUAGES

Pupils at Ellerton speak at least seven languages other than English and Afrikaans. These include the African languages of Xhosa, Zulu, and Sotho.

"There are 23 children in my class. We are lucky because in some of the other classes there are about 40. We sit in groups of six."

Sbongile's maths book

MURALS

The school is decorated with bright murals. Sbongile loves Ellerton, but when she first joined she felt the rules were very strict.

" In the playground we play four blocks and cops and robbers. But my favourites are games with a tennis ball, which I play with my friends."

Sbongile's picture

ASSEMBLY

There is an assembly once a week where the children sing their school song and the national anthem. Lessons include maths, English, Afrikaans, science, and history. Sbongile's favourite is science because there is so much to learn.

"Sometimes in our class we bake and make snacks. In music we sing songs. We also do computers, art, and library lessons. In summer we swim in the school's swimming pool."

Sbongile and her friends

Maria

For six years, girls in Afghanistan were not allowed to go to school at all. Now things have changed. Maria attends a girls' school in Kabul run by the new government with help from UNICEF.

LIFE IN AFGHANISTAN

In 2002, a new government came to power in Afghanistan. Since then, there have been schools and educational opportunities for women. Maria was lucky that there were schools she could go to by the time she reached school age.

 ..."During the time I was too young to go to school I studied at home. My older sister Tamana helped me learn how to read and write."

Afghanistan

Fewer than one in five women (and one in two men) can read in Afghanistan. Now, under a new government, much more schooling is available for girls.

AN EARLY START

Maria has to get up early so she can be at school by 7 a.m. She wears the school uniform, a smart black tunic and trousers with a white headscarf.

..."It takes 30 minutes to walk to school from our house. I go to school with two of my sisters. My brothers go to a different school."

TIME FOR LEARNING
The girls sit on a rug during classes. Maria sits next to her best friend, Hafiza. She studies hard because she would like to become a teacher.

... "My favourite subject is Dari (Afghan Persian), which is the language that we speak. I find it easy."

FUN WITH FRIENDS
Maria plays with her friends and also eats a snack she has brought from home. Maria's school is only for girls.

... "I like to play jump rope during break, but my favourite thing about school is playing football!"

A GIFT FROM UNICEF
Every child at Maria's school received a special school bag and exercise books from UNICEF.

School bag

School books

... "Two of my wishes are to have a new house and to stay in Kabul."

م / ک

Maria's name in Dari

"I want to be a teacher."

Every child has the right to

play

running, jumping, collecting,

A serious business

Playing is actually very important.
You don't need expensive toys, just a good imagination.
Kids don't need to speak the same language to play together.
Sports exercise your body, team games teach you to work
with other people, and play that involves pretending
lets you use your imagination.

pretending, imagining, laughing

What's the point of playing?

Play might not seem like an essential activity, but it is. Playing is the main way children prepare for growing up.

- **Playing on your own** teaches you to think for yourself and to enjoy your own company.
- **Playing with others** teaches you to get along with other people and work well in a group.
- **Playing allows you** to be creative and enables you to explore the world around you safely.
- **Playing trains you** to be resourceful and to use your imagination.

pretending, acting, singing,

Many children don't get the chance to play.

- You have to **work** long hours.

- It is too **polluted, dirty, or unsafe** outside.

- **There is a war,** or a war has recently ended.

- You have **suffered** mentally or emotionally.

How many different ways to play can you think of?

- **You can play by yourself** by jumping on your bed, reading a book, dressing up, or keeping a diary.

- **You can make things** by drawing or painting, building a model aeroplane, baking a cake, or making a monster.

- **You can take part in sports.** Team sports like football or netball teach you how to get along with others. Gymnastics, running, and swimming teach you to rely on yourself. All sports help keep you fit and healthy.

- **You can have a hobby** like collecting stickers or rocks, playing an instrument, doing magic tricks, or looking after a pet.

- **You can play with others** in the playground, in the park, using board games, or by inventing your own games.

You don't need toys to play, but you do need time and a place to be by yourself or with your friends.

Adults keep out!

It's hard to play with adults looking over your shoulder.

All children are entitled to their privacy.

building, hiding, seeking, chasing, painting

That's because it's hard to play when:

- You have **no energy** because you don't get enough food to eat.

- There is **not enough room** to play inside your house.

- You have to **look after** your younger brothers and sisters all the time.

- You are physically **ill.**

Playing can be messy!

Just playing

Children are the experts when it comes to playing! Indoors or outdoors, whether or not there are toys to play with, kids can always find a way to keep busy and have fun.

South Africa Children are playing in a playground in King William's Town.

Botswana Playing a game called *Makaroo*, a boy sits in the middle of a circle of chairs while other boys run around him.

.... There are games that you can only play when there are lots of people to have fun with. What other games can you think of that require a lot of players?

.... Jumping around is fun and makes you feel good, but it can tire you out.

Philippines Building blocks and jigsaw puzzles demand quietness and concentration. It's easy to become very absorbed in this type of play.

 ... Sometimes it's nice to play near other people without actually playing with them. You can share ideas but still do things your own way.

Peru Look at how this boy is using his whole body. Football involves all of you, not just your feet and a ball!

 ... Football is probably the most popular game in the world.

Kenya This Somali boy holds a toy bus he created out of paper and card. It took a lot of time and imagination to make this toy.

 ... You can play by making something, and then you can play with the thing you've made!

Cuba Three Ukrainian boys play chess at a camp providing medical assistance to children who have suffered exposure to radiation.

 ... A game of chess can take hours because the players spend so much time thinking carefully about the moves they will make.

Michael

A sheep and cattle station in the South Australian outback is home to Michael, his sister, and their parents. Because he lives so far from a school, Michael does his schoolwork alone and talks to his teacher over a two-way radio.

AUSTRALIA

Australia
Australia's population is small in relation to its size. Some farming families live hundreds of kilometres from their neighbours.

ANIMALS
As well as cattle and sheep, there are other animals on the station. The family keep *chooks* (chickens) for their eggs and ducks for their meat. There are dogs and also horses used for *mustering* (rounding up) the cattle.

..... *"I help feed and water the dogs, chooks, ducks, horses, and cattle. When I grow up, I would like my own cattle station so I could be like Dad."*

OUTDOORS

Michael spends a lot of time outdoors. He loves taking the dogs for a run and riding his bike around the station. Twice a year he goes to camp where he meets other children his age.

SHEEP

There are 1,200 sheep and 550 cattle on the ranch. Once a year, the sheep are sheared for their wool. Even Michael and Rebecca get involved, although most of the work is done by hired sheep hands.

... "I talk to my friend, Naish, on the school radio after lessons. He lives on Bulgunnia Station, 630 km (390 miles) from here."

Michael's favourite book

... "The best things about living in the outback are the windmills, the open spaces, and sunsets. The worst thing is not being able to see my friends."

Michael's favourite teddy

AUSSIE RULES

The ball is kicked in Aussie Rules football, but players are also allowed to catch and run with it. Michael and Rebecca practise, but they can't play a real game – you need two teams of 18 players for that!

TOYS AND GAMES

Michael plays on his own with his toys – trucks, tractors, and a motorbike. He loves reading *Outback Magazine,* and he also watches television and plays games on his computer.

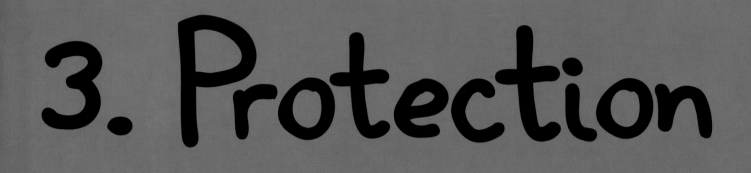

3. Protection

Every child should have someone to **love** and **care** for them.

Every child should be protected from **work** that could harm or exploit them.

Protection – noun; to protect – verb 1 to defend or guard from attack, invasion, loss, insult, etc.; cover; shield from harm.

Disability should not prevent any
child from participating fully in life.

Children need protection from the

fighting and destruction of **War**.

Every child needs

love and care

love, care, hugs, support,

Someone to look after you

Children need the support of caring adults.
It's often parents who have this job, but not always.
Adult carers should do whatever is best for the child.
Every child needs an adult who can listen to them,
comfort them when they are hurt or sad,
and encourage them to be sensitive to others.

safety, laughter, company

Who loves and cares for you?

Everyone needs someone to look after them.

- **You don't just share** a home with the people you live with – you also share your life with them. They love you and look after you.

- **Children can live** with mothers, fathers, aunts, uncles, cousins, bigger brothers or sisters, grandparents, step-parents, foster parents, adoptive parents, parents' girlfriends or boyfriends, or just friends.

- **Your family** can consist of just one other person, or 20. They can be young or old, male or female – the important thing is that they care for you.

Love makes the world go round.

They cook your **dinner** and make you eat up all your **greens**.

They ask if you have got any **homework** to do and try to **help** you do it.

Before you could read, they told you **bedtime stories** and **sang** to you.

Mothers, grandmothers, aunts, cousins, stepmothers, foster mothers, adoptive mothers, carers

Big brothers let you play with them.

Little brothers give you hugs and kisses.

Some families can't look after their children because of...

• Poverty Some families are overwhelmed by poverty and just can't afford to care for all of their children. In such a situation a child might have to leave home to find work.

• Death When parents die, children often go to live with relatives. If no one can take care of orphaned children, they may end up homeless.

• War In the 1990s, more than 1 million children were orphaned or separated from their families by war. Organizations such as UNICEF help to reunite them.

• Violence in the home is an awful reality for some. Child victims of violence may run away and end up living on the streets.

What then?

The government makes sure that these children are looked after by providing orphanages or foster homes for them, or by finding adoptive parents.

Growing up alone

More than 13 million children under 15 have lost one or both parents to AIDS.

At least 1 million children a year are left motherless by death in childbirth.

Millions of children live on their own on the streets of the world's cities.

Think what your family does for you.

They usually buy you the **clothes** and **shoes** you wear.

They make you **tidy** your room and tell you when to **go to bed**!

They try to **help** you in every way they can.

Fathers, grandfathers, uncles, cousins, stepfathers, foster fathers, adoptive fathers, carers

Big sisters let you play with them.

Little sisters give you hugs and kisses.

Family feelings

Just like people, families come in different shapes and sizes. Family members are often related to one another, but they don't have to be. It also doesn't matter how many there are in your family as long as you all support and love each other.

Burundi Terrible fighting has raged in Burundi, leaving many orphans. A woman called Maggy opened a foster home where she looks after all the children in the photograph below.

... Children who are temporarily without a home may live in foster care. Eventually, they might return home or be adopted permanently by a new family.

Lesotho This mother and her son live in a centre run by Catholic nuns. There are more than 40 young women living there, some of whom have children of their own. The women learn skills and produce goods that are sold at the local market.

... Some parents no longer live together. Their children normally live with either their mother or their father, but typically they may visit their other parent.

UK This family consists of a mother, a father, and a child whom they have adopted. Children whose parents are dead or unable to care for them may be permanently adopted by a new family. People who want to adopt children have to be checked out to make sure they will be good parents.

... It's all right for adopted children to think about their biological parents sometimes, even if they are happy and secure with their adoptive family.

Pakistan Families where several generations live together are common in many countries. In Pakistan, when a man gets married, his bride usually joins him in his parents' home. Their children grow up surrounded by aunts, uncles, and cousins.

... In a large family like this, you never need a babysitter because there is always someone around to help look after the children!

China This is a small family. It consists of two parents and just one child.

... China is slightly smaller than the USA, but it contains more than four times as many people. It is a very densely populated country.

Finland There are 20 children in the Oikarinen family – 6 sons and 14 daughters. Their ages range from 3 to 27 years old.

... The average number of children in a Finnish family is just 1.8, but Bertta and Seppo Oikarinen belong to a religious movement that encourages people to have large families.

Ivana

Until two years ago, Ivana lived in an institution for children and adults. Some residents had mental disabilities or mental illnesses, some were physically disabled, and some had no disabilities. Conditions were bad, and few people received the care they needed.

Yugoslavia

After years of war in the Balkans, peace has returned to Kosovo and it is being rebuilt. Most of its residents are Kosovar Albanians.

CHILDREN'S HOME

When she was 10, Ivana came to live in a brand-new children's home with just eight other children and caring staff.

... "I stay up late to talk and to play with my toys together with Marina and Jasmina, my room-mates. They are my best friends. I am very happy in my new home."

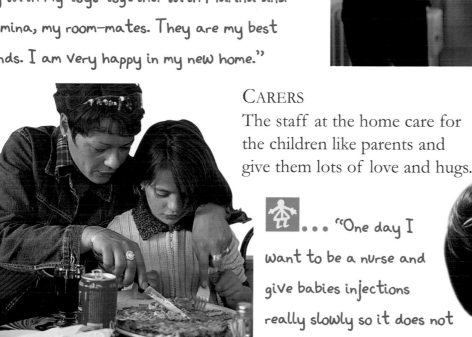

CARERS

The staff at the home care for the children like parents and give them lots of love and hugs.

... "One day I want to be a nurse and give babies injections really slowly so it does not hurt them and they don't cry."

SCHOOL

Ivana received no education in the institution. Since coming to live in the home, she has started attending the local primary school.

... "I like school, but not when there is too much homework and I don't have time to play with my friends in the home."

"All my toys are good!"

No child should be exploited through

Work

tiring, low wages, long hours,

Working for a living

Most adults have to work to earn money.
Many children have to work to help their family.
When children work, they don't have time for other things.
Work can be a fun and important part of growing up, but no
work should be harmful or take the place of learning, playing,
and having time to enjoy being a child.

boring, no free time, exploitation

Why do children work?

More than **210 million** children aged between five and 14 work for a living. More than half work in dangerous jobs. Children often work long hours for little pay in poor conditions.

• Most children who work full time do it to help their families. Even when children are not well paid, their income can make a big difference.

• Child workers are deprived of the simple joys of childhood and are forced into a life of drudgery.

• Many businesses employ young children because they can be paid very little or nothing at all and can be easily taken advantage of.

• Some work is dangerous and can lead to stunted growth and accidents.

• Some part-time work is all right for children.

• It is important to know the difference between child labour that takes advantage of children and work that does them no harm.

Not all work is bad for children.

Some types of work can be all right if –
- You are not too young for the job
- You can stop any time you want to
- It does not interfere with school or play
- You are paid a proper wage
- It is not dangerous to your physical or mental health
- You have time to spend with your family
- You are treated fairly and have someone to complain to if you are not.

Working is wrong when –
- You are too young for the job
- It involves unsafe or harmful work or working conditions
- You cannot stop when you want to
- There is little or no pay
- It prevents you from going to school or takes the place of school
- It separates you from your family
- You are treated unfairly or abused.

Problems with child labour

Some types of labour are not acceptable for children and should not be tolerated anywhere.

Many children never get the chance just to be children.

- **73 million working children** are under 10. In the short term, they miss out on education, and in the long term, they are more likely to die early.

- In Brazil, Kenya, and Mexico, at least one in four farm workers is **under 15 years old.**

- Sometimes children **as young as eight** are taken to other countries to work.

- Children often work the **longest hours** and are the **worst treated** of all labourers.

- Millions of girls work long hours as **domestic labourers** in private homes where beatings and harassment are common.

- In sub-Saharan Africa, **23 per cent of all children** between the ages of 5 and 14 work.

Hard work

Most countries have laws that limit the hours children are allowed to work and control the age at which they can work full time. The major reason for these laws is that children already have work to do – school work – and that is what should come first.

Ecuador Rosita, like one third of Ecuador's population, works in agriculture. Here, she helps to harvest wheat. It is extremely hard work if done by hand and not by machine.

...Agricultural work is often seasonal. At harvest time, schools in farming areas may close down so that children can help their families to gather in the crops.

Mauritania Mame Diara is an orphan living with her cousins. She does most of the household chores, including cleaning, cooking, and looking after the family's animals.

👧... When we think about child labour, we often forget that millions of children are not working in fields or factories but in private homes.

UK Douglas lives on his dad's farm. He helps out whenever he is not at school. His main job is feeding the family's three sheepdogs and two pet dogs.

👧... The kind of work that Douglas does is not exploitative. Children in the UK are allowed to work a few hours a day as long as the work does not harm them and their education is not affected.

Iraq Ten-year-old Dana sells sweets on a street in Erbil. Dana does not earn very much money for the long hours he works. He also runs the risk of falling sick or of being robbed.

👧... Apart from missing out on their education, child workers on the streets are also easy targets for criminals. These children are vulnerable to violence and abuse.

Arif

A special programme has given Arif, who lives in a slum, the chance to work as a reporter on a television show for, by, and about children. The show, *Mukta Khabor*, has allowed Arif to excel.

NEPAL

INDIA

INDIA

BANGLADESH

MYANMAR

Bangladesh

Sixty per cent of people in Bangladesh do not have enough money to live on. Almost 25 per cent of the population are between 12 and 17 years old.

RICKSHAW WORKSHOP

Like many other slum children, Arif had a job as well as attending school. It was hard work and very poorly paid.

 ... "My hands used to really ache after days of work painting rickshaws. Now things are very different."

Bicycle rickshaw

CHILD REPORTER

The young crew of *Mukta Khabor* research, report, and run the newsroom entirely on their own. They have become role models for other young Bangladeshis.

Mukta Khabor logo

PAINTING

Arif discovered he had a talent for art and became a good painter through his job at the rickshaw workshop. He still enjoys painting in his free time.

... "I like it when local people tell my parents they saw me on television."

... "I earn four times more than in my old job, and I learn new things every day."

FAMILY

Arif has three brothers – Sharif is nine, Rajiv is seven, and Raju is four. Arif is happy that he can help his family with the money he earns from *Mukta Khabor*.

Arif's art

... "If I were president, I would help parents so they don't have to send their children to work."

COMMUNAL KITCHEN

Arif's mother prepares a meal of fish in the kitchen the family shares with other families. Everyone in the family eats together.

No child should fight in a

War

danger, confusion, fear,

Not for kids

War is a fact of life for many children.

War uproots families and destroys communities.

After a war, children need help rebuilding their lives.

Children are the most innocent victims of war. They are sometimes even dragged into wars and forced to fight against their will. These children are robbed of their childhood.

machines, soldiers, destruction

What happens in a war?

No child ever started a war, but children
fight and die in wars **every day**.
No child should have to live through a war.

- **Normal life** is impossible during war. Communities
break down when people are forced to leave their
homes, and schools and hospitals are destroyed.

- **Families** are damaged by war. Children may become
separated from their families. Many people are killed
or injured, both physically and emotionally.

- **The damage** continues long after the war is over.
Children and their families must somehow put
their lives back together and learn how to live
normally again.

War is not a game.

During the 1990s, more than **2 million children** died in wars.

28 million women and children had to flee.

Armed conflicts are raging in more than **30 countries**.

6 million children have wounds from war.

Children have the right to be protected from the dangers of war.

War kills, but it also destroys normal life
in many other ways.

PERIGO MINAS!
DANGER MINES

• **War destroys life.** Most of the people who die or are injured in war are not soldiers but ordinary people, who cannot fight back. It is women, children, and elderly people who suffer the most.

• **War destroys homes.** During war, people are forced to leave their homes and their countries and become refugees. Often, they never come back. Wars have made millions of children homeless.

• **War destroys childhood.** Children who have seen horrible things respond in different ways. Some may feel depressed or hopeless about the future. Others might become angry or violent.

• **War destroys play.** Long after a war is over, land-mines buried in schools, playgrounds, and fields continue to wound or kill children and adults.

Facts about land-mines

Each year, more than 10,000 children are killed or hurt by land-mines.

Children are at risk from land-mines in 90 countries.

A land-mine can cost less than $3 to manufacture – and $1,000 to find and dispose of safely.

In war, innocent people suffer.

Millions more died from hunger and disease caused by war.

Many of them never return to their homes.

Around 300,000 children are fighting in wars.

Land-mines kill or injure nearly 30 children every day.

Children affected by war may need help to recover.

War and recovery

War is bad for everyone but particularly for innocent children. How do wars and conflicts affect children? And how are children helped to recover after the fighting ends?

Hands linked, these former child soldiers board a UN aeroplane that will take them to a better life.

Sudan During the civil war, these children were forced to become soldiers. Now they are being flown to transit centres where they will receive health care, education, and counselling to help them recover from their experiences. UNICEF and other organizations will make every effort to trace their families. It is hoped that they will soon be able to return home and resume a normal life.

Leaving war behind The real work begins after the fighting has stopped. Homes and communities are rebuilt and families reunited. Schools re-open and children begin to catch up on what they have missed.

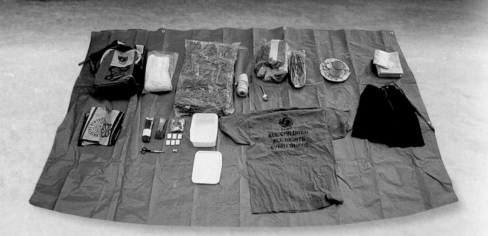

Recovery kit A kit containing high-protein biscuits, bandages, school supplies, and a T-shirt saying "All Children. All Rights. Everywhere" is given to former Sudanese child soldiers to help them get back to normal.

Rwanda These boys from Rwanda have survived the fighting. Now they are receiving support to help them deal with their wartime experiences. Here, in a trauma treatment centre run with UNICEF support, they wield fake guns that they have made themselves and act out some of the things they have witnessed.

☖ ••• This family was separated during war but has been reunited with help from aid agencies.

Angola Although the war is now over, danger still lurks just beneath the surface. This man teaches children in a displaced persons' camp to beware of buried land-mines. It is estimated that there are still between 10 and 15 million unexploded land-mines in Angola, and as many as 50–100 million unexploded land-mines scattered in countries throughout the world.

Deactivated land-mines

☖ ••• Land-mines are very cruel weapons. Most injuries are suffered by civilians long after the conflict is over.

Yugoslavia A child refugee from Kosovo holds an umbrella over his mother, who is cradling her younger child in her arms. The family is waiting to board a bus that will take them to safety in neighbouring Albania. Having left home in a hurry, these refugees, like many others, have abandoned their homes and most of their possessions.

☖ ••• Families frequently become separated in the rush to escape a conflict. UNICEF works to reunite these children and their parents.

Names have been changed to protect the people involved.

... "I like football. If I don't become a doctor, I might want to become a professional footballer."

Isa

During the war in Sierra Leone, some fighters came to Isa's house and took him away. After two years, he was released, along with other children caught up in the war. He is now back home.

BACK TOGETHER AGAIN

An organization called Caritas looked after Isa for a year. Then he went back to his family. Isa recently went to a Christmas party organized by Caritas.

... "I have two brothers called T-Boy and Yasuf and two sisters called Sally and Kai. My new baby sister, Marie, is just five months old. I also play with my cousins, who are called Momoh, Jeneba, and Fatu."

Sierra Leone

Raging civil war in Sierra Leone resulted in many deaths. Almost one in three people fled from their homes.

GUINEA

SIERRA LEONE

LIBERIA

PLAYING WITH FRIENDS

Isa has no toys of his own, but there are always children around to play with.

... "I like playing draughts with my best friend, Brima. Another game we play is called balancing ball."

Playing balancing ball

HARVEST TIME

Nobody plants crops during a war because they might have to leave before the food can be harvested. Now that there is peace, Isa has planted some groundnuts.

... "I would like to help my country because a lot has been destroyed and needs rebuilding."

"I want to be a doctor."

TIME FOR SCHOOL

Wearing his school uniform and reading a book, Isa walks with his father. At school Isa studies maths, English, geography, social studies, and the Bible.

... "I lost three years of school because of the fighting. I am now 10 years old, and I am really happy at the school I go to. My favourite subject is English."

No child should be held back by a

disability

respect, opportunity, patience,

Enjoying a good life

We all deserve the chance to do our best.
Disabled people may need some extra help.
Help starts with understanding and caring.
We can't always prevent people from being disabled,
but we can make sure that disabled people have the
same opportunities as everyone else.

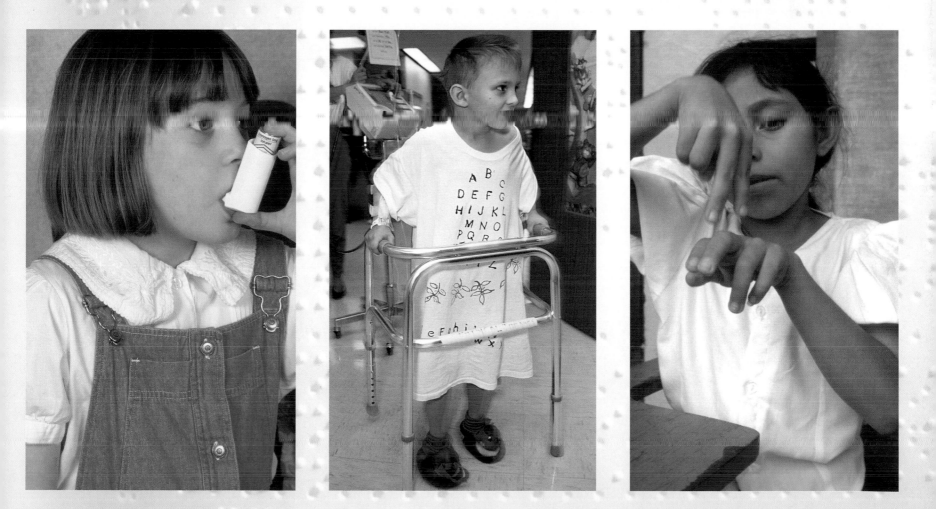

encouragement, understanding

What is life like with a disability?

Imagine trying to move around if your legs didn't work, or to communicate if you couldn't hear or see clearly.

● **Children** who are disabled are just like everyone else except that some parts of their bodies do not work very well. Disabled children can lead normal, full, wonderful lives as long as they receive the right kind of support.

● The biggest **problem** that disabled children face is when people do not understand their needs. Letting disabled children speak, and listening to what they have to say, are the best ways to help them.

Disability can have some effect on your life.

● Sometimes disabled children need **equipment**.

● **Training** and **education** can help disabled people.

● **Operations** and **medicines** help some disabilities.

● Disabled people want to be **treated normally**.

A disability can be many things. It can be –

- **Physical** – a difficulty with part of the body.

- **Mental** – some disabilities make it hard to think.

- **Visible** – such as a missing limb, or the inability to walk.

- **Invisible** – such as deafness or dyslexia.

Disability can happen in many ways.

- Some children are **born** disabled. Some children are disabled in **accidents**.

- Some children are disabled by **war**. Some children are disabled by **disease**.

Children with **disabilities** should not be discriminated against. They should be given equal treatment, education, jobs, and a chance to lead **normal lives**.

Or it can affect your life a lot.

They may use **hearing aids** or **artificial limbs**.

Blind people can learn to use a **guide dog**.

An **operation** may help repair a damaged limb.

What you can do to help

Always be patient and understanding with people who may need extra help.

Volunteer to help someone with a disability.

Never make fun of anyone with a disability.

Living with a disability

Having a disability does not neccessarily mean you can't see, speak, hear, or walk – it may just take a bit more effort to do things. Doctors can sometimes help to ease a disability, but most disabled people cope by being resourceful and finding alternative ways of doing things. Like everyone else, they appreciate people behaving considerately towards them.

Cuba Julia was two when she caught an infection that led to an eye condition. She was almost blind when an operation on the *Orbis* teaching eye hospital restored her sight. It's a very unusual hospital because it's actually on board an aeroplane.

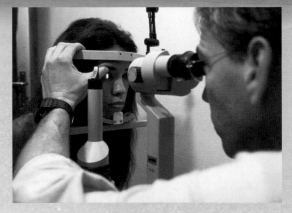

... The plane travels with a crew of volunteer doctors. In each country, they perform surgery with up to 50 local doctors watching. This way, the local doctors learn how to perform the same life-changing operations.

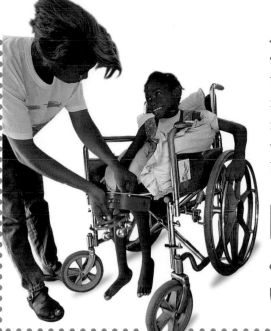

Jamaica This little girl cannot walk, but that doesn't mean she needs help to move around. The metal rails on the back of her wheelchair allow her to be mobile by using her arms.

... When there is a problem with one part of the body, another part may be able to take over its job.

Romania Using a mirror, a speech therapist at a kindergarten helps a child practise speaking. There are many different reasons why people might find it difficult to speak. They might be hard of hearing, or have difficulty controlling the muscles that are responsible for speech, or perhaps the part of their brain that deals with speech has been damaged.

... With help and encouragement, children who find it difficult to speak clearly, or to talk at all, can improve their language skills and speak more confidently.

Nicaragua Deaf people may learn to use sign language to communicate with one another. Sign language differs from country to country.

... Deaf people may also learn to read lips. By watching the mouth of the person speaking, they can work out what words are being said.

Yugoslavia Burim from Kosovo lost his legs in an accident, but he is learning to walk again using artificial legs and a walking frame. Eventually, he hopes to be able to walk on his new legs unaided.

... Physically disabled people can participate and excel in sports. The very best disabled athletes compete in the world-class Paralympic Games.

CJ

When he was five, CJ – of Atlanta, Georgia, USA – was knocked down by a car. He had to re-learn how to walk, talk, and even eat. These days, despite some mental disabilities, CJ is a keen football player.

FAMILY SUPPORT

CJ's family are proud of his sporting skills. They always come to support him when he plays in a football match.

... "CJ has overcome a lot to get where he is today. He doesn't let anything deter him. He is a blessed child." – CJ's mother

RECOVERY

CJ's parents were told he wouldn't be able to recognize them when he woke from his coma, but he knew who they were straightaway.

CANADA

USA

Atlanta •

MEXICO

USA

The United States of America is the third largest country in the world in both physical size and population.

LOCAL NEWS

Therapy: Focus on patients and families

Back from the brink

Helping hands: At the rehabilitation unit of Scottish Rite Children's Medical Center, parents of injured children are key to any recovery.

By Ellen Whitford

Love gives a helping hand

SPECIAL OLYMPICS

CJ plays football with the Special Olympics. It runs sports events worldwide for people with mental disabilities.

... "Our football team is called the Trickum Tigers. I like being the defender, and I like getting a chance to kick the ball."

FOOTBALL FANS

Although not as popular as some other sports, many people in the USA play football. In 1994, the country even hosted the World Cup.

... "There are eight kids on my team. We practise every morning. We play against other kids at tournaments."

CJ's football boots

LOOKING TO THE FUTURE

CJ has recovered well from his accident but he still goes to physical therapy at the local hospital and has speech therapy lessons at school.

... "I want to be a fireman so I can help people when there is a fire in their house."

SPORTING TROPHIES

As well as football, CJ has received trophies in recent years for playing baseball, basketball, and bowling.

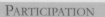

4. Participation

Every child has the right to an **identity**

including a name, nationality, and religion.

Participation – noun; to participate – verb **1** to take part or to share with others. **2** to form a partnership with others. **3** sharing benefits.

Every child has the right to freedom of

expression.

A good **life**, lived to its full potential, is the right of every child.

Every child has the right to an

identity

name, nationality, religion,

Who am I?

Everyone needs to belong to a community.
Some children are excluded from a community because they
do not have a name or a nationality.
When you have a name, a nationality, and the right
to practise your religion, you can fully participate in
the life of your country and community.

family, culture, community

Who are you?

What is your name? Where are you from? What religion do you practise? No one should be able to take your identity from you.

Your **name** is special.
What does it mean to you?

- **Your name** might mean something in the language you speak or in a language that is part of your religion or culture.

- **Your name** may have been chosen for you by someone in your family or by a leader of your community.

- **Your name** connects you to members of your family and your community, both to those living and those who have died.

- **Your name** is a part of you. People should respect you by making the effort to call you by your correct name.

People should be free to

There are many different religions – such as Christianity, Islam, Judaism, Hinduism, and Buddhism.

Each religion has its own teachings – Jews have the Torah. Hindus have the Vedas. Muslims have the Koran.

Every religion has different holidays – Muslims celebrate Eid ul-Fitr. Buddhists celebrate Wesak Day.

Each religion has its own holy places – Buddhists have Lhasa. Sikhs have Amritsar. Muslims have Mecca.

Each religion has different forms of worship – some use silence, some use spoken prayers or chanting.

Everyone is born somewhere, so why doesn't everyone have a nationality?

• **Sometimes children** do not get registered when they are born because their parents are afraid of going to the government offices.

• **Sometimes children** become refugees because of war. When this happens, they may have to live in another country where they do not have any nationality.

• **Sometimes governments** take away the nationality of certain people in their country. Often this is caused by war, and often it causes war.

• **Sometimes governments** deny nationality to people who belong to a particular ethnic group.

What can governments do?

Find all the children who are not registered and grant them nationality. Recognize everyone born in that country as a citizen. Help all refugees to return home.

practise all religions.

Other religions include Sikhism, Rastafarianism, Zoroastrianism, Bahai, Jainism, and many others besides.

Christians have the Bible. Sikhs have the Guru Granth Sahib. Buddhists have the Thripitaka.

Hindus celebrate Diwali. Christians celebrate Christmas. Sikhs celebrate Baisakhi. Jews celebrate Passover.

Christians, Jews, and Muslims have Jerusalem. Hindus have Varanasi. Roman Catholic Christians have Rome.

Some religions use singing or dancing, some use meditation, some use special foods, some light candles.

What's in a name?

Your name is an important part of your identity. It is part of who you are, and it is one way that other people know you. Can you imagine what your life would be like if you did not have a name? Children's names are special to them and to their parents.

What does your name mean?

... "Bilal is a gentle name and it was the name of the first person who said the call to prayer."

Bilal's parents wanted a name that would reflect his Muslim religion, so they named him Bilal, after a companion of the prophet Mohammed.

Jasleen and **Ravina** are friends. Their names are from the Punjabi language. Jasleen means "divine princess". Ravina means a "strong, free spirit".

... "My parents chose the name Ravina for me because they expected me to be strong, with a free spirit and character. My parents also named me after a famous river called the River Ravi."

Paul The name Paul originally meant "little". In the Bible, St Paul was a leader of the early Christian church.

... "My name doesn't mean anything special to my parents. They just liked the sound of it."

Junique In Junique's family, her name means "very special".

... "My dad thought I was unique, so he put a J in front of unique to make Junique. Both my parents agreed on my name."

... "My parents liked the sound of the name Mark, so that's what they called me."

Mark was a very important person in the Bible. He wrote about Jesus' life in one of the four gospels.

Meena means "princess". Her parents named her Meena because she was special, just like a princess.

... "I like my name. It makes me feel special."

Meegan is an old English word that means "strong". Meegan's middle name is Timothea, which means "honouring God".

... "I like my name. My parents want me to live up to the meaning of my name."

Teresa In Chinese, the name Teresa sounds the same as the word for "happy".

... "My mother named me Teresa because she was very happy when I was born."

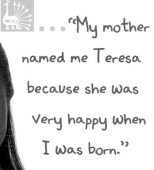

TERESA

Haresh is a Hindi name. The first part of Haresh's name, "Har", means God.

... "When I was a few months old, my parents went to the Temple and the priest picked the letter H, so my parents gave me a name starting with H."

Nationality

All nations and peoples are unique and special. Having a nationality means that you have the protection and benefits of a country. It also means that you share a culture and a history with the other people in your country.

Bangladesh A young country, Bangladesh separated from Pakistan and finally became independent in 1971 after a long civil war. Today, Bangladesh is a vibrant country.

••• Children participate in their country's "Say Yes for Children" campaign. The campaign aims to build support for the policies that will improve and protect the lives of children.

UK In Northern Ireland, Stephen, Ruairi, and Connell are proud of their Irish culture and support their local Gaelic football team.

••• Gaelic football is an ancient Irish sport where teams of players try to punch, bounce, or kick a ball into or over a net.

Peru The majority of people in Peru are South American Indians, descendants of the Incas who once ruled Peru.

••• The Peruvian mountains are home to many millions of Indians who still speak the local language of Quechua and maintain a traditional way of life.

Spain Uxue lives in Santander, the capital city of a small province in northern Spain, called Cantabria. This region is very close to the northern provinces of the Basque Country, where the people have a completely unique language and culture.

••• The regions of northern Spain are very different from those further south. In Cantabria, it is more mountainous and not so sunny. It is beautiful.

South Africa Many different people live in South Africa. As well as various local ethnic groups, South Africa is also home to people whose parents and grandparents emigrated from Europe and India.

••• South Africa has 11 official languages. There are nine African languages, as well as Afrikaans and English, which were brought by the Dutch and British settlers who came in the 19th century.

Najaha and Abdisukri

Najaha and Abdisukri are sister and brother. Their family came to the Netherlands from Somalia as refugees. They are now happy to think of themselves as Somali children living in the Netherlands.

The Netherlands

The Dutch people who live in the Netherlands have a long history of welcoming refugees and people in need.

THE NETHERLANDS

GERMANY

BELGIUM

ADJUSTING TO A NEW HOME
At school, Najaha and Abdisukri play with children from many different countries. Because they were young when they left Somalia, they have found it easy to adjust to life in the Netherlands.

..."I like the Netherlands, but I don't like the weather. It's always raining and it's too cold!"

Family photographs of Abdisukri and Najaha

TWO LANGUAGES
Abdisukri and Najaha speak Somali when they are at home with their family, but most of the time they speak Dutch, the language of the Netherlands.

FOOTBALL FUN
Abdisukri plays football with a famous football club near his home. It is called Willem II.

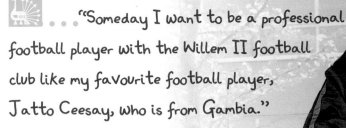

... "Someday I want to be a professional football player with the Willem II football club like my favourite football player, Jatto Ceesay, who is from Gambia."

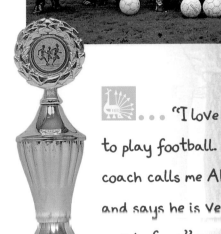

DAILY PRAYERS
Abdisukri and Najaha's family is Muslim. The whole family prays five times a day. They also go to the mosque together, where they meet some of their friends.

A plate with verses from the Koran

... "I love to play football. My coach calls me Abdi and says he is very proud of me."

Abdisukri's football trophy

SCHOOL TIME
Najaha enjoys mathematics, reading, writing stories – and going to the amusement park! Study is important to Najaha because she wants to become a lawyer.

... "I don't have any best friends. All my friends are my best friends."

Najaha's school books

"Our favourite food is samosas."

FAVOURITE FOOD
At home, the family eats Somali food. *Samosas* are fried pancakes stuffed with meat and vegetables.

Religion

Each religion means something very special to those who practise it. That is why it is important that no one is prevented from following a religion or faith.

Jewish *Torah* scroll and pointer   Tibetan Buddhist prayer wheel

South Korea Eyes shut to aid their concentration, these children pray during Sunday school at a large Pentecostal church.

... In South Korea, about half the people are Christian and half are Buddhist.

Myanmar At the *shinbyu* ceremony, boys enter a Buddhist monastery for a short time. When they are older, they may decide to become monks.

USA These girls are singing in a Gospel Church choir. Gospel music is very lively. The singers often clap and sway while they are singing because they feel so excited about praising God.

 ... Gospel music has its roots in songs that Africans brought to America as slaves and sang while they worked.

Christian cross   Islamic tile   Sikh *nishan sahib* symbol   Ganesh, a Hindu god

India During a coming-of-age ceremony, young boys are given a sacred shirt and a thread to wear throughout their lives. This boy has now become a full member of the Parsi (Zoroastrian) community.

... The boys dress like royal princes in the days of the first Buddhist priests, more than 2,000 years ago. It is a proud day for their parents.

... The sacred thread, called the *kusti*, is wrapped three times around the waist. It represents three important things to remember – good thoughts, good deeds, and good words.

A NEW LIFE

Eli's family spent two years arranging the move to Israel. Eli was scared but also curious about his new life.

Eli

Eli came to Israel from Uzbekistan in the former Soviet Union. His family are Jewish, but Eli didn't know very much about Jewish beliefs or practices before he came to live in Israel.

Israel

Jews from all over the world have chosen to make Israel their home, though people of other faiths live in Israel, too.

YEMIN ORDE

Many of Eli's classmates live at Yemin Orde Youth Village because they came to Israel without their parents. They learn about Judaism in school and also participate in Jewish activities outside school hours. Every Saturday they celebrate *Shabbat*, the Jewish sabbath.

... "My school is called Yemin Orde. I chose to come here so I could learn more about being Jewish."

DIFFERENT BACKGROUNDS

Children at Yemin Orde come from more than 20 different countries including Ethiopia, Russia and the former Soviet Union, Brazil, Mexico, Colombia, Slovakia, Bosnia, Romania, Morocco, India, France, Italy, Great Britain, Martinique, and Israel!

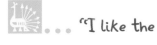 "It's really interesting meeting children from so many countries. We are all Jews, but we have different traditions, which we share with each other at Yemin Orde."

TORAH

Eli studies the *Torah* – the Jewish holy book – in Hebrew, but he also has a translation into Russian to help him understand it better.

"I like the special atmosphere on Shabbat. Sometimes I spend it with my family. We say some blessings at home, but I don't always go the synagogue."

Torah

Tefillin, containing verses from the *Torah*

PRAYER

There is a beautiful synagogue at Yemin Orde. To pray, Eli wears a skullcap called a *kippa*, a shawl called a *tallit*, and *tefillin*, which are little boxes containing verses from the *Torah*.

"At school, we are encouraged but not forced to pray every day. I love finding out about my religion."

Kippa

Every child has the right to free

expression

opinions, contribution, respect,

Saying and doing

Show how much you care and take an interest.
Expressing yourself means getting involved.
There are millions of ways to express yourself.
By expressing ourselves we share things we like and
dislike, and how we think and feel. This is an
opportunity to learn about ourselves and others.

participation, individuality, input

Express yourself!

What **opinions** and **ideas** do you have? Do you think they are important? Well, you're right, they are important. Your **opinions** and **ideas** could change the world.

● The world is a **great**, **fun**, **scary**, **happy**, **sad**, **wonderful**, **exciting** place – but it could be better. Is there a problem in your school, town, country – or in another country – that you think you could help solve?

● Everyone has the **right** to express an opinion, not just adults but children, too. Children who **cannot** express their opinions may feel frustrated about living in a world they can't change.

How many ways can you think of to express yourself?

● Children had their say at the UN Special Session on Children, held at the United Nations Headquarters in New York in May 2002. This was a chance for children from around the globe to talk to world leaders about issues affecting them.

Take action
and help make the world a better place by
expressing your opinions and **participating**.

• **Think of** something you would like to see improved, or a problem you would like to see solved. It can be in your school, your city, or somewhere far away.

• **Find out** all you can about that problem and tell your friends about it too. You could make contact with groups that are already working to fix it.

• **Think about** how you, as a child, can help solve that problem. For example, you might not have money, but you can encourage adults to give money to help.

• **Choose** one way to help. It can be a small thing, such as not wasting resources, or something bigger, such as starting your own organization.

Getting adults to listen

Agree a time with parents and teachers when they can listen to your concerns.

Try to bring along some facts to back up your opinions.

Allow your parents and teachers to respond to what you say.

Keep calm and treat people with respect.

Protect our wildlife

HELP SAVE DOLPHINS

world peace

• **Creating art** – draw, paint, sculpt, photograph, film, record, write. You can share what you make with others.

• **Participating** – recycle cans and bottles, pick up rubbish in the streets, organize a clean-up in a local park.

• **Talking** – listen to what others have to say and tell them what you think. Try seeing things differently.

• **Making friends** – every time you meet someone new, you can share new ideas and thoughts with that person.

• **Sharing** – other children may have the same problem or concern as you. Together, you could fix it.

Freedom of expression

Human beings make speeches, write stories, paint pictures, compose and sing songs, perform dances, and act in plays. Sometimes we express ourselves because we have strong feelings or thoughts about something and we want to share them with other people. Sometimes we express ourselves because we feel we need to. Whatever the reason, self-expression is something to enjoy and take pride in.

Brazil These children, members of EDISCA dance school, discuss the production they are rehearsing. The show is about people who live in a rubbish dump. The children in the dance troupe come from deprived communities themselves.

 ... Everyone has to work hard in a dance troupe. While this dancer balances in a strikingly graceful pose, another member works just as hard to support her there.

Brazil Diego stands in front of a mural he painted of Bob Marley, a Jamaican reggae musician. Artists frequently work alone, but a big work of art like this can involve many people.

. . . This mural means that Diego's work can be seen and appreciated by many people. It also makes the neighbourhood much more colourful.

Botswana These girls are recording their discussion about AIDS for a radio programme. AIDS is a big problem in Africa, and this programme is a good way to get information about the disease out to young people.

Bolivia A young boy learns to play the guitar, a traditional instrument of the Andes. The musical notes are written down in his exercise book.

. . . Once you can play an instrument, it's great fun to try and play with other musicians.

. . . Self–expression includes art, dance, and music, but words are important too. Children must speak out about things they care about or that affect them.

Taralyn

"I play hand drums and clackers for traditional drumming, singing, and dancing. I think I'll always enjoy doing that."

Taralyn attends Chief Leschi School near Seattle in the USA. The Puyallup tribe of Native Americans runs the school, but pupils come from more than 60 Native American tribes. They study English, maths, and many other subjects, as well as learning all about different tribal traditions.

CANADA

Seattle

USA

MEXICO

USA

Before Europeans arrived in America 400 years ago, the land was home to hundreds of Native American tribes.

LANGUAGES
Some children speak a Native American language, but classes are in English.

SACRED LAND
The school is constructed around a sacred circle of land that stayed untouched throughout the building process. Students and teachers do not enter this area, but many school buildings look onto it.

"You can see Mount Rainier from our school. There are eagles that like to fly over our school. I think that is special too."

CIRCLE TIME

Every day there is an opportunity for children to sing traditional songs, do some drumming, and learn about each other's tribes during Circle Time.

"I like Circle best because we get to sing, drum, and dance. Sometimes we also have special guests and storytelling."

"Powwows are social celebrations. They don't belong to our historical tradition, but to that of the Plains tribes. We love to join in anyway."

CULTURE DAY

The school holds an annual celebration of Native American traditions. Local people are invited to join in the dancing. All year the children make gifts, which they finally give away during Culture Day.

STORY POLE

There are several story poles in the school grounds. Each one illustrates a particular legend and took months to carve.

"In the main entrance to our school, we have a story pole that tells how the Puyallup River was formed by two black whales after a great flood."

SALMON FEAST

Living near the coast, the Puyallup tribe traditionally enjoyed salmon as one of its staple foods. There's always a big salmon barbecue on Culture Day.

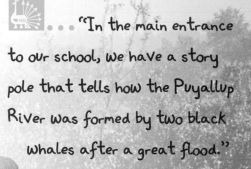

Every child deserves a happy

life

dreams, wishes, ambitions, aims,

Aim high!

The future is in your hands.

You can make a better world.

What are your wishes for the future?

All around the world, children like you are working to improve their communities. If we all work together, we can create a world where there is a happy life for everyone.

achievements, hope, happiness

Sibasish

The World Health Organization, UNICEF, and other partners are trying to wipe out polio. Sibasish is a team leader in a project that teaches people living in slums in Kolkata (Calcutta), India, about the disease and encourages families to vaccinate their children against it.

POLIO KILLS

A highly infectious disease, polio mostly affects poor children under five years old. Polio can be transmitted through food or water. It starts with the same symptoms as the flu, but it sometimes leads to paralysis and, rarely, death.

"We walk down the streets with posters. Mine says: 'Get vaccinated and lead a good life.' We play music and sing songs to get the message out."

Polio vaccine

HOUSE TO HOUSE

Sibasish talks about polio and invites people to attend an immunization day when their children can be vaccinated. Most are very happy to be protected against the disease and don't need much persuasion.

India

More than a billion people live in India, making it the world's second most populated country. The climate ranges from tropical monsoon in the south to temperate in the north.

"We go on campaigns three times a week to all the homes with children under five. We teach people about polio and the importance of the vaccination."

THE CAMPAIGN AGAINST POLIO

It is a privilege to be involved in the campaign. Local children train as campaigners each year. In addition to learning about polio, they learn to be good communicators and leaders.

"Sometimes we go to people who are not in a good mood and they throw us out. We don't give up. Instead, we go back again a day or two later when they have calmed down and tell them about polio."

Colorful charts

Campaign bag

"Each child campaigner gets a special bag. We have fun making charts and posters, which we carry in these bags and use when we campaign."

IMMUNIZATION DAY

The work pays off on immunization day. The campaigners do a final round, making sure that parents are taking their children to be vaccinated.

"We want a world free from polio."

"I want to do good for other human beings and give every child a better tomorrow."

TAKING THE VACCINE

A health worker gives a child the vaccine. It is usually two drops of liquid on the tongue. To be completely effective, four separate doses must be taken.

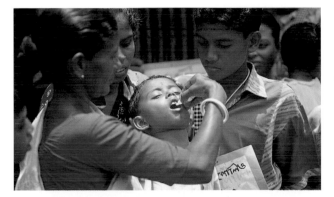

Mayerly

Mayerly is one of the leaders of the Children's Movement for Peace in Colombia – the children's response to the violence in their country. The Movement has been nominated for a Nobel Peace Prize three times.

THE CHILDREN'S MOVEMENT FOR PEACE

The Movement began when Mayerly was invited to a meeting with children from various organizations. Her best friend, Milton, had recently been killed in a fight between youth gangs. The children decided it was time for the violence to be stopped.

. . . *"We are tired of violence. We have the right to be children, and the right not to be afraid to go out."*

Colombia

Civil war has been ravaging Colombia for more than 40 years. This has unsettled the lives of millions of children.

PANAMA

VENEZUELA

COLOMBIA

ECUADOR

BRAZIL

PERU

LEARNING ABOUT PEACE

The symbol of the Children's Movement for Peace is the white hand seen on books, T-shirts, and banners. The Movement includes more than 100,000 children. They play games and support one another instead of joining violent gangs and becoming involved with weapons and drugs.

... "The white hand means no to violence."

... The banner proclaims "I am a peace-builder" – the dove of peace flies over the Colombian flag.

PEACE-BUILDERS

The Movement believes that Colombia's children deserve the right to live, the right to peace, the right to love, and the right to safety for themselves and their families. Parades like these have helped the government to ban the recruitment of children under the age of 18, into the Colombian army.

MAYERLY'S MUM

Mayerly's parents were worried that she might be harmed for her involvement in the Movement. Now they are very proud of their daughter.

... "We are convincing children in our schools and people in our neighbourhoods that this is the way to a better future. No one can kill 10 million Colombians who speak about peace."

"We build peace with play and friendship."

Index

Acknowledgements

DK would like to thank:

All the children and their parents who participated in the book, particularly: Anita McDaniel; Jacqueline Mliswa; and Raili Jones.

The staff of UNICEF and the staff of UNICEF National Committees in all the countries we visited and the people working with them, particularly: Sara Cameron, Siddharth Dube, Hirut Gebre-Egziabher, Patricia Lone, Jan Mun, Tina Omari, Hashi Roberts, Ellen Tolmie, Nicole Toutounji (New York); Chulho Hyun (Afghanistan); Naseem-Ur Rehman (Bangladesh); Rochita Talukdar (India); Susan Aitkin (Laos); Bert Tielemans (Netherlands); Monica Awad (Occupied Palestinian Territory); Cyriaque Ngoboka (Rwanda); Donald Robertshaw (Sierra Leone); Nance Webber (Sudan); Andy Bool (UK); Patrick Fruchet (Yugoslavia).

All of the schools, teachers and organizations who assisted us, particularly: Deborah Allen, Tami Cooper, Erika Hope (Chief Leschi School); Laura Buller (US consultant); Tony Ackerman (Ellerton School); Michelle Berriedale-Johnson (Allergy Action); Lewsey Park Pool (UK); Planet Ice (UK); Sharon Knight (Wilbury Junior School, Letchworth, UK); Lisa Leblanc (Special Olympics, Georgia, USA); Sacha Kamau and Zoe Horner (The Travel Company, London); Tamsin Maunder (WaterAid); Chaim Peri, Susan Weijel (Yemin Orde, Israel); Cristina and Alex Zampalo.

All of the people at Dorling Kindersley, particularly: Jacqueline Gooden, Tory Gordon-Harris, Cheryl Telfer (design assistance); Abbie Collinson (map artworks); Penny Arlon, Caroline Bingham, Simon Holland, Rebecca Knowles, Cynthia O'Neill (editorial assistance); Jane Oliver-Jedrzejak (jacket editor); Jenny Cavill, Kristen L'huede, Mariza O'Keeffe (administration); David Roberts (cartography); Alex Kirkham (licensing); Sarah Mills, Gemma Woodward, Hayley Smith, Claire Bowers (picture library); Rosie Adams (DK Australia); Shuka Jain, Kiran Mohan (photography co-ordination, DK India).

Chris Bernstein (index); Lorrie Mack (proofreading).

The photographers: Shome Basu (India), Andy Crawford (Netherlands, Spain, UK, USA), Jim Holmes (Laos), Roger Lemoyne (Israel, Occupied Palestinian Territory), Leon Mead (Australia), Shehzad Noorani (Bangladesh, Sudan, Yugoslavia), Rod Shone (UK), Jon Spaull (Rwanda, Sierra Leone), Asad Zaidi (Afghanistan).

The publisher would like to thank the following for their kind permission to reproduce their photographs:

a=above; b=below; c=centre; l=left; r=right; t=top;

Andes Press Agency: 56bl, 57bl, 75bc, 90bl, 90br, 114bc; Lisa Payne 107tr; Carlos Reyes-Manzo 60tr, 100bl; **Art Directors & TRIP:** 30bl; H Rogers 111tc; **John Birdsall Photo Library:** 71cl; **Corbis:** 30-31, 51tr, 74br, 77, 84tr, 90, 91bl, 103tr, 110bl, 115bc; Owen Franken 19c; Julie Houck 39bc; Richard Hutchings 22tr; Joel W Rogers 39br; Michael S Yamashita 18br; **Jane Cumberbatch:** 45tr, 46br; **Earth Images:** 12tr; **Getty Images:** 69tr, 90c; **Getty Images News Service:** 68tl, 82-3, 100-1; Don Smetzer 93br; **Glasgow Museum:** 103bc; **Hutchison Library:** 71tr, 71cr; **Images Of Africa Photobank:** 30bl; **Impact Photos:** 122-123; **Jewish Museum:** 110tr; **Joods Historisch Museum:** 102br; **Magnum:** 4tc, 4tr, 5tr, 8tr, 23tc, 23tr, 23tr, 30bc, 44tl, 44tr, 44tcl, 44tcr, 45tl, 45tcl, 46bl, 46bc, 47bl, 47bc, 56bc, 56br, 57bc, 57br, 64tl, 64tc, 66bl, 66bc, 66br, 67bl, 67bc, 70cr, 74bc, 75bl, 75br, 76tl, 83bc, 91br, 94tr, 94cr, 94br, 94l, 95bl, 100bc, 101bl, 101br, 110cl, 110-1, 111cr; Daniel Alan Harvey 98tc1, 114br; Steve Moss 122br; **Masterfile UK:** 66-7; **Network Photographers Ltd.:** Jenny

Matthews 67br; **Panos Pictures:** 71bl; **Pictorial Press Ltd:** 65tcl; **Pictor International:** 11br, 58, 74-5, 91bc; **Powell Cotton Museum:** 102bl; **Powerstock Photolibrary:** 18-19; **Save the Children:** 19bl; Neil Cooper 47br; **Science Photo Library:** 38-9; **Still Pictures:** 87c; Shehzad Noorani 10bl, 10br; Hirimui Schwarzbach 10bc; **Peter Stone:** 65tr; © **UNICEF:** Blid Alsbirk 15r, 95br; Cindy Andrew 18c; Patricio Baeza 119br; Alejandro Balaguer 61bl, 76cr; David Barbour 61br; Liza Barrie 93tl; Radhika Chalasani 87br,123r; Franck Charton 64tr, 74l; John Chiasson 122l; Stephanie Colvey 41cl; Donna DeCesare 6bc, 99br, 126c, 127br; Lauren Goodsmith 64ctl, 79cl, 79bl; Jeremy Horner 50cl, 50bl, 78c, 98tr, 115r, 126br, 127tl, 127tr, 127c, 127cr, 127bl; Altaf Hossain 106c; Roger Lemoyne 14c, 14l, 22bl, 30tr, 30br, 36c, 36l, 37r, 39br, 41bc, 65tl, 82l, 82c, 82r, 83l, 95c, left back end paper; Stevie Mann 65tc, 86c, 86t, 86bl, 86br; Susan Markisz 116bc; Ruby Mera 98tcr, 114bl; Shehzad Noorani 9tr, 41ct, 50tr, 50br, 61tl; Giacomo Pirozzi 8tl, 8tcl, 8tcr, 9tc, 11l, 23r, 28tr, 40l, 41cr, 51r, 60bc, 61cr, 70bl, 79bl, 85tr, 87t, 99tr, 101c, 107br, 115br, 119bl; Betty Press 87cl; Nicole Toutounji 83r, 84bc, 85bc; Claudio Versiani 99tcl, 99tcr, 118c, 118tr, 119tl.

Jacket: **Corbis:** Tim Page front cl; **Getty Images:** Brian Bailey front tll; Wayne Eastep front trr; Dan Kenyon front bl; David Roth front br; **Barnabas & Anabel Kindersley:** back tl, tr, cl, cr, front b; **Magnum:** Abbas front tl; Ian Berry front tcr, tcrr; Harry Gruyaert front tc, Peter Marlow front bc; Chris Steele-Perkins front cr; **The Photographers' Library:** inside back; **Planetary Visions:** inside front bl; **Save the Children:** back bl, bcr; Neil Cooper back br; **Still Pictures:** Hirimui Schwarzbach spine t; © **UNICEF:** Radhika Chalasani back bcl; Nancy McGirr front tr.

All other images © Dorling Kindersley.

For further information see: www.dkimages.com